FELLA ALWAYS SA[...]
LOVE THAT'S NOT [...]
MA USETA MAKE [...]
FOR WHEN YOU GO ON THE BATTER WIT[...]
IRISH SLANG THAT MAKES A HOLY SHOW[...]
[...]TS FOR GOBDAWS AS THICK AS MANURE [...]
[...]ISH SLANG THAT'S GREAT CRAIC FOR C[...]
[...]H QUOTATIONS SOME SMART FECKER IN [...]
[...]K OF IRISH SONGS YER OUL' FELLA ALW[...]
[...]CKIN' BOOK OF IRISH SEX & LOVE THAT'S[...]
[...]UVELY IRISH RECIPES YER MA USETA M[...]
[...]BOOK OF IRISH SAYINGS FOR WHEN YO[...]
[...]E 2ND FECKIN' BOOK OF IRISH SLANG T[...]
[...]CKIN' BOOK OF IRISH INSULTS FOR GOBD[...]
[...]L THE BOOK OF FECKIN' IRISH SLANG TH[...]
[...]E BOOK OF DEADLY IRISH QUOTATIONS S[...]
[...]N' ON ABOUT THE BOOK OF IRISH SONGS [...]
[...]D AT A HOOLEY THE FECKIN' BOOK OF I[...]
[...]S EYES THE BOOK OF LUVELY IRISH REC[...]
[...]URRIER THE FECKIN' BOOK OF IRISH SAY[...]
[...]VER OF SAVAGES THE 2ND FECKIN' BOO[...]
[...]E FIRST ONE THE FECKIN' BOOK OF I[...]
[...]AND ONLY HALF AS USEFUL THE BOO[...]
[...]TE HOORS AND BOWSIES THE BOOK OF [...]

D0323555

The book of feckin' Irish Slang that's great craic for cute hoors and bowsies

*JANEY MACK!
IT'S A FECKIN' NUMBER ONE
BESTSELLER*

The Feckin' Collection

The book of feckin' Irish Slang that's great craic for cute hoors and bowsies

Colin Murphy & Donal O'Dea

THE O'BRIEN PRESS
DUBLIN

First published 2004 by The O'Brien Press Ltd,
12 Terenure Road East, Rathgar, Dublin 6, Ireland.
Tel: +353 1 4923333; Fax: +353 1 4922777
E-mail: books@obrien.ie Website: www.obrien.ie
Reprinted 2004 (three times), 2005, 2006, 2007, 2008.

ISBN: 978-0-086278-829-2

British Library Cataloguing-in-Publication Data
Murphy, Colin
The book of feckin' Irish slang that's great craic for cute
hoors and bowsies. - (Feckin' collection ; bk.2)
1. English language - Ireland - Slang
I.Title II.O'Dea, Donal
427.9'415

8 9 10 11 12
08 09 10

Printing: Reálszisztéma Dabas Printing House, Hungary

What's the story?

'Did you hear that the scrubber and the wagon were plastered last night and ended up in a mill? It was deadly!'

This sentence makes perfect sense to most Irish people. But to everyone else on the planet it means the following:

'Did you hear that the cleaning utensil and the four wheeled horse-drawn vehicle were covered in a lime/sand/water mixture and then transported to a processing factory, with fatal consequences.'

This book sets out to avoid any such confusion arising in the future by explaining in clear and precise terms the meaning of a vast number of commonly used Irish slang words or expressions. If you, dear reader, believe that any of the listed phrases have been incorrectly translated, please feel free to go and ask my arse.

Acting
the Maggot (expression)

Fooling about in a
somewhat boisterous
manner.
*(usage) 'Anto! Will you
stop acting de maggot
and give the oul' wan
back her wheelchair.'*

Arseways (adj)

Mishmash. Complete
disarray. Total mess.
*(usage) 'Me car has
been arseways since I
ran over the pedestrian.'*

Ask me arse (v)(rhetorical)

What do you take me for, a silly billy?
(usage) 'Lend YOU a fiver? Go and ask me arse!'

Bad dose (n)

Severe illness.
(usage) 'I'd a bad dose of the scutters after them ten pints of Guinness last night.'

Bags (n)

(see also Hames)

A botched job.
(usage) 'The hairdresser made a right bags of me perm.'

Bang on (adj)

Correct. Perfectly accurate.
(usage) *'That shot ye took at the ref's groin was bang on.'*

Banjaxed (adj)

(see also Knackered)

Broken. Severely damaged.
(usage) *'Me marriage to Deco is completely banjaxed.'*

Barrel (v)

Hurry. Race. Rush.
(usage) '*When the Guards arrived, the Minister for Justice barrelled out of the Lap Dancing Club.*'

BIFFO

(acronym)

Big Ignorant Fucker From Offaly.
(usage) '*Em, excuse me BIFFO, would you mind not using the table cloth as a hanky?*'

Black Stuff (n)

Stout.
(usage) '*Nine pints of the black stuff and a gin and tonic for de mot please.*'

Blarney (n)

Nonsense talk used to charm foreigners. *(eg) 'They say the ghost of Finn Mac Cumhall still stalks the Grand Canal. Buy another round and I'll tell you all about it, my American friend.'*

BLATHER...BLATHER...

Blather (n) (v)

Empty, worthless talk. *(usage) 'What are ye blatherin' on about, Taoiseach?'*

Bogtrotter (n)
(see also BIFFO, Culchie, Mucksavage, Mulchie)

A person of rural extraction. *(usage) 'And that, my bogtrotter friend, is what we call electricity.'*

Bollixed (adj)

(*see also* Fluthered, Gee-eyed, Langered, Ossified, Paralytic, Plastered, Rat-arsed)

Somewhat in excess of the legal alcohol driving limit.
(usage) 'After twelve pints I was a bit bollixed.'

Bowsie (n)

Person (esp. male) of very disreputable character. A useless good-for-nothing.
(usage) 'Is there anyone in the Government who isn't a bleedin' bowsie?'

Boyo (n)

Male juvenile
(esp. delinquent).
*(usage) 'Y'know sarge,
I think dem boyos
outside the off-licence
are up to no good with
dem crowbars and
flick-knives.'*

Brasser (n)

A lady of the night.
*(usage) 'As a judge, it's
my job to keep brassers
like you off the street.
So get into the bloody
car!'*

Brutal (adj)

Awful, terrible, hideous.
(usage) 'The head on her was brutal.'

Bucketing down (v)

Raining cats and dogs.
(usage) 'Sure it's bucketing down outside. Might as well have another six pints.'

Caught rapid (expression)

Caught in the act. Proven guilty beyond doubt.
(usage) 'I was caught rapid in bed with me mistress by me bit on the side.'

Chiseller (n)

Young child.
(usage) 'That slapper's only eighteen and she's already had three chisellers.'

Clatter (v)(n)

To slap playfully with palm.
(usage) 'I only gave him one little clatter, yer Honour. His skull musta been brittle.'

Cod (v)

(see also Let on)

To pull one's leg in a jovial fashion.
(usage) 'Ah, sure I was only coddin'. Your wife wasn't electrocuted at all.'

Craic (n)

(Pronounced crack)

Fun.

(usage) 'There's great craic to be found in that pub on the corner.'

(Note: Misinterpretation of this expression has led to several arrests of foreign visitors who were caught trying to purchase a particular illicit drug.)

Culchie (n)

(see also BIFFO, Bogtrotter, Mucksavage, Mulchie)

A person whose birthplace is beyond Dublin city limits.

(usage) Q: 'What d'ye call a culchie in a stretch Limo?'

A: 'The deceased.'

Cute hoor (n)

Suspiciously resourceful gentleman.

(usage) 'Speaking from his yacht off Bermuda, the cute hoor denied he'd made any payments to politicians in return for favourable building contracts.'

Deadly (adj)

Great, brilliant, fantastic.

'Yer woman's got a deadly arse.'

Dense (adj)

Stupid. Thick.
(usage) 'My accountant and solicitor say that paying tax is dense.'

Desperate (adj)

(Pronounced despera)   Dreadful, awful.
'Yer man's arse is desperate after a few pints.'

Diddies (n)

Extremely childish term for a woman's breasts.
(usage) 'Counsel for the defence has got a magnificent pair of diddies, hasn't she m'Lud?'

Donkey's Years (n)

Inordinately long time. An epoch. Time immemorial.
(eg) Period of time people of Ireland have been waiting for a National Soccer Stadium.

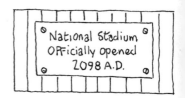

National Stadium Officially opened 2098 A.D.

Doss (on the) (n)

Failure to attend school/work during specified hours.
'I swear I wasn't on de doss. I really did have leukaemia yesterday.'

Dosser (n)

Person with a relaxed attitude to attendance at his/her place of employment.
(eg) Dosser: 'Hey Mick, will ye move dis piano for me while I go an get me medicine in dat chemist, beside dat pub?'

Drawers (n)

Knickers. Panties.
(usage) 'You could fit a hurling team into me wife's drawers. In fact I think she does on a regular basis.'

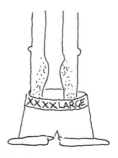

19

Dry Shite (n)

Someone of limited verbal/social skills. *(usage) 'There was a dry shite on the seat beside me at the client party.'*

Eat the head off (v)

To rebuke verbally in an aggressive manner. *(usage) 'The missus ate de head off me just because I puked into de back of the TV.'*

Eccer (n)

Homework *(usage) 'Hey, Ma. Do me eccer for me or I'll tell Da about the postman.'*

Eejit (n)

Person of limited
mental capacity.
Incapable fool.
Complete moron.
Imbecile.
*(eg) Person(s) responsible
for Ireland's health
service.*

Effin' and blindin' (expression)

Swearing profusely.
*(usage) 'The Taoiscach
was effin' and blindin'
because the new
Government jet didn't
have the Playboy
Channel.'*

Eff off (v)

Restrained/polite swear word used in refined Irish society. *(usage) 'Father, those chappies on the factory floor told me to 'eff off' when I inquired if they'd made my morning tea.'*

I SAY OLD SPORT, ANY CHANCE OF A QUICK EFF?

Fair play! (expression)

Well done! *(usage) 'Fair play te ye for gettin' de leg over Deirdre.'*

Fanny (n)

Female genitals.

(usage) 'That Deirdre's fanny was as tight as camel's hole in a sandstorm.'

(Warning: Some American visitors have inadvertently caused shock or offence through the mistaken belief that 'fanny' refers to buttocks, as it does in the US. eg 'After that bike ride, I feel like giving my fanny a good rub,' may raise some eyebrows if spoken aloud in public.)

OH FECK, I SAID F*CK!!!

Feck (v)(n)

Politically correct term for f**k.

(usage) 'Ah feck off Father Murphy. You're nothing but a feckin' fecker.'

Fierce (adj)

Very. Extremely.
*(usage) 'I had a fierce
bad headache after
drinking Deirdre's
perfume.'*

Fine Thing (n)
(see also Ride)

An attractive
man or woman.
*(usage) 'She looks like
a fine thing after seven
pints.'*

Flahulach (adj)
(Pronounced
Flah-hule-uck)

Generous.
*(usage) 'The
councillor was feeling
flahulach after he got
his bribe from the
property developer.'*

Fluthered (adj)

(see also Bollixed, Gee-eyed, Langered, Ossified, Paralytic, Plastered, Rat-arsed.)

Having a high blood/ alcohol ratio. *(usage) 'I was so fluthered last night I slept with the missus.'*

Fooster (v)

Not getting much done. Fiddling about. *(usage) 'Will ye stop foosterin' about Mick and stamp on the goalie's face!'*

Full shilling (adj)

(not the)

Mentally challenged. Not fully sane. Nuts. *(eg) Anyone who attempts to commute by means of public transport in Dublin or Cork on a regular basis is said to be 'not the full shilling'.*

GAA
HEADQUARTERS
NO FOREIGN SPORTS
ALLOWED
(EXCEPT AMERICAN FOOTBALL
WHICH BRINGS IN LOADSA
WONGA).

Gaa (n)

Sport played by the G.A.A. (Gaelic Athletic Association). *(usage) 'Gaa is a great game. It's just a shame about the G.A.A.'*

Gaff (n)

Home. Place of
residence.
*(usage) 'Dat's some
gaff yer woman de
President has in de
Phoenix Park.*

Gammy (adj)

Damaged. Crooked.
Useless.
*(usage) 'The entire
Cabinet is gammy.'*

ARE WE
HAVING GOOSE
FOR DINNER?

I'LL JUST
HAVE A
GANDER

Gander (n)

A quick glance.
*(usage) 'I'd give
anything for a gander
at Noleen in the nip.'*

Ganky (adj)

Repulsive. Ugly.
*(usage) Q. What's the
difference between a
ganky-looking girl and
an absolute ride?
A. About ten pints!*

NOW THAT'S
WHAT I CALL A
GANSEY LOAD!

Gansey-load (adj)

Many. Lots. An excess.
*(usage) 'There's a
gansey-load of dossers
in the Dáil.'*

Gargle (n) (v)

Drink (alcohol)
*(usage) The Cabinet
single-handedly
prevented the closure
of the brewery by
retiring to the Dáil bar
for a 'gargle or two'.*

Gas (adj)

Amusing. Funny.
Hilarious.
(usage) *'It was gas
when Cormac broke his
collar-bone.'*

Gawk (v)

To stare rudely.
(usage) *'What are you
gawking at ye ignorant
gobshite?'*

Gee (n)

Female reproductive
organ.
(usage) *'I've a pain in
me gee trying to get
laid tonight.'*

Geebag (n)

Woman of unpleasant character.
(usage) 'Me wife's a right geebag.'

Gee-Eyed (adj)

(see also Bollixed, Langered, Ossified Paralytic, Plastered, Rat-arsed)

Having partaken of large quantity of ales/spirits.
(orig) *Subject was so inebriated that his eyes have shifted from the normal horizontal orientation.*

Get off with (v)

Be successful with a
romantic advance.
*(usage) 'I got off with
four different fellas at
the Christmas party.'*

I'D LOVE TO GET
OFF WITH YER MAN

HE'S MY
HUSBAND

Go and shite!

(expression)
(see also Ask me
Arse, Get up the
Yard)

I am not in
agreement with your
suggestion.
*(usage) 'The priest
told me to abstain
from bad language, so
I told him to go and
shite!'*

Gobdaw (n)

(see also Gobshite)

Person of restricted mental ability.
(usage) 'The Minister for Finance is a complete gobdaw.'

Gobshite (n)

(see also Gobdaw)

Person of below average IQ. Socially inept individual.
(usage) 'The Minister for Finance is a complete gobshite.'

Gollier (n)

A mass of phlegm expelled from mouth at high speed.
(usage) 'I landed a gollier in the geography teacher's coffee.'

Gombeen man (n)

Petty, snivelling, fawning underling.
(eg) Chief executive of any Irish semi-state company.

WHATEVER YOU SAY, MINISTER...

Gouger (n)

Aggressive, repulsive person.
(usage) 'Do you really take this gouger to be your lawful wedded husband?'

Guff (n)

Feeble excuses. Blatant lies.
(eg) 'Sorry I'm late, boss. I had to take me Ma to the hospital for her spine replacement operation.'

Gurrier (n)

Hooligan. Delinquent.
Ruffian.
(usage) *'Give the oul'
lad back his teeth, ye
little gurrier!'*

Hames (n)

Complete mess.
(usage) *'The plastic
surgeon made a hames
of me arse.'*

Head-the-ball (n)

Term of address: 'you'.
(usage) *'Hey, head-the-
ball, how do I get to
Donegal?'*

HEY HEAD THE BALL!!! KICK I

Heavin' (adj):

Thoroughly packed.
*(usage) 'In the
planning trial the
defendant's box was
heavin' with County
Councillors.'*

Hockeyed (v)

Heavily defeated.
*(usage) 'Ireland
hockeyed Brazil five-nil
in the World Cup Final,
and then me bleedin'
missus woke me up.'*

Hole (n)

Anus.
*(usage) 'Piles are a
pain in the hole.'*

Holy Joe (n)

Self-righteous, sanctimonious hypocrite.
(usage) If Holy Joes a *so holy, how come there's always so man* *of them queuing for confession?*

PLEASE GOD, CAN
THERE BE WORLD
PEACE AND CAN I
HAVE A NEW CAR

Holy show (expression)

Disgrace. Spectacle.
(usage) 'Me Ma mac *a holy show of hersel* *when she dropped he* *pint into the baptisme* *font.'*

Hooley (n)

Raucous celebration involving drinking and singing.

(usage) ' ... and folks, I'm asked to invite you all to a hooley in Murphy's pub immediately after Mick's funeral.'

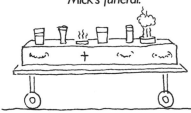

Hop (v)

Play truant from school.

(usage) 'Let's go on the hop and get pissed. I'm fed up teaching those bleedin' kids anyway.'

Howaya (greeting)

Hello. Hi.
(usage) 'Howaya, ye big bollix!'

How's she cuttin'? (expression)

How is life, my good friend?
(usage) 'How's she cuttin', yer honour?'

How's the craic? (expression)

How are you? What's happening?
(usage) 'How's the craic, Deirdre?'

I will in me arse/ bollix/hole/fanny (expression)

I absolutely refuse to
do what you suggest.
(usage) 'Marry you? I
will in me bollix!'

MICK I WANT YOU TO
HAVE THE SNIP!

I WILL IN ME BOLLIX!

Jackeen (n)

A rural person's
derogatory name for
a Dubliner.
(usage) Q: 'What
does a Jackeen say on
his first day in work?'
A: 'What do I do
now, Daddy?'

Jacks (n)

Toilet, restroom.
(usage) *'Ye tink dat's bad? Wait 'til ye see de state of de jacks in de Dáil.'*

I WOULDN'T GO IN THERE.
THE MINISTER'S GOT
VERBAL DIARRHOEA.

DAIL TOILETS

Jammers (adj)

Extremely crowded.
(usage) *'The Dáil bar is permanently jammers.'*

Jammy (adj)

Exceedingly lucky.
(usage) *'The jammy bastard won the Lotto again.'*

Janey Mack! (expression)

Expression of utter disbelief. Wow!
(usage) *'Janey Mack! That politician told the truth!'*

Jar (n)

Pint of beer or stout.
(usage) *'I'm dying for a jar. The court will adjourn until 2pm.'*

Jaysus! (expression)

Jesus Christ!
(usage) 'Ah Jaysus, ye puked in me pint!'

Jo Maxi (n)

Taxi. Cab.
(usage) 'Eh hello. I'd like a Jo Maxi please to collect four people from Madame Le Whip's Maison de Plaisir and take us back to Government Buildings.

Joe Soap (n)

Anybody. Somebody. Nondescript person.
(usage) 'I shagged some Joe Soap last night.'

WHAT ARE YOU GOING TO CALL HIM, MRS SOAP?

JOE!

Kick the shite out of (v)

Violently assault, causing actual bodily harm.
(usage) *'Right lads, we're down 2-0. Let's kick the shite out of dem.'*

Kip (n)

A place/establishment of poor repute.
A dump.
(usage) *'Benidorm is a kip.'*

Knackered (adj)
(see also Banjaxed)

Very tired. Broken beyond repair.
(usage) *'My arse was banjaxed after that vindaloo.'*

Knockers (n)

Mammaries. Breasts.
(usage) 'Are dem
knockers real, missus?'

SO YOU'VE FINALLY
HAD THE JOB DONE
ON YOUR KNOCKERS

YEAH, I HAD THEM
REDUCED.

Langer (n)

Male reproductive
organ.
(usage)
*Countrywoman A: 'This
carrot reminds me of
me husband's langer.'*
*Countrywoman B: 'Ye
mean the size of it?'*
*Countrywoman A: 'No.
The dirt of it.'*

Langered (adj)

(see also Bollixed, Ossified, Paralytic, Fluthered, Gee-eyed, Plastered, Rat-arsed)

Very drunk.
(usage) 'I was so langered I woke up with a kebab in me knickers.'

Lash (v)

To rain heavily.
(usage) 'We had two weeks' holiday in the sunny south-east and it never stopped bleedin' lashin'.'

Leg it (v)

To flee rapidly. To run away.
(usage) 'Let's leg it before the waiter comes back with the bill, Sarge.'

Loaf (v)

To head-butt.
(usage) 'Righ', Murphy.
As a bouncer, your
primary job is to loaf
everyone who tries to
get into this bleedin'
nightclub.'

Manky (adj)

Disgustingly filthy.
(eg) Any street, waterway,
public toilet, or beauty
spot in Ireland.

Massive (adj)

Great. Fantastic.
(usage) 'Look at the
tiny little arse on yer
woman. It's massive!'

Mentaller (n)

Nut case. Looney.
(usage) Politician:
'Commissioner, about
1000 of the Gardai are
complete mentallers!"
Commissioner:'I know,
it's just not enough, is it?'

Me oul' segotia

(expression)

Term of endearment.
My old flower.
(usage) 'Any chance of
a ride, me oul' segotia?'

Mill (n)(v)

Fight. Public brawl.
(usage) 'Hey, look
lads! A mill between
wimmin'!'

Mitch (v)

(see also Hop)

To play truant. To skip school.

(usage) 'Honest, we're not mitchin', Guard. We're doin' a project on juvenile alcohol consumption.'

DON'T WORRY BARMAN, OF COURSE WE'RE OVER 18!

Mortified (adj)

(see also Scarlet)

Highly embarrassed.
(usage) 'I was mortified when the baby came out black.'

Mot (n)

Girlfriend.
(usage) 'Me mot drinks tequila sunrises like there's no tomorrow.'

Muck savage (n)

(see also BIFFO, Culchie, Mulchie)

Country fellow lacking in sophistication.
(usage) 'No, you big muck savage, you may not eat curry chips in the delivery room.'

Mulchie (n)

(see also BIFFO, Culchie, Muck savage.)

Person from a small rural town.
(usage) 'That, my mulchie friend, is a three-storey building.'

BE THE HOKEY, WOULDYA LOOK AT THE SIZE OF THAT.

Murder (adj)

Very difficult. Almost impossible.
(usage) 'Getting a Cavan man to buy his round is murder.'

49

Nip (in the) (adj)

Nude. Naked.
*(usage) 'The doctor
examined me in the nip.
Whatever happened to
his clothes is anyone's
guess.'*

IT'S OKAY. I'M A
DOCTOR. I'M USE
TO SEEING NAKE
WOMEN.

Nixer (n)

Job done on the side,
for cash, thus avoiding
tax. *(usage) 'Tell you
what, I'll write your next
Budget speech as a
nixer, Minister.'*

Oul' wan (n)

Mother.
*(usage) 'Me oul' wan
had me when she was
sixteen.'*

Oul' fella (n)

Father.
(usage) 'Me oul' fella hasn't been seen since.'

Oirish (n)

Mythical language and culture used by Americans and British when portraying Irish people.
(eg) 'Top of de mornin' te ye, be de hokey. D'ye happen te know, me good sir, where I'd be findin' a leprechaun dis fine day, at all at all?'

Ossified (adj)

(see also Bollixed Fluthered, Gee-eyed, Langered Paralytic, Rat-arsed.)

Totally inebriated.
(usage) 'Do you know it takes just three pints to get an Englishman ossified?'

THREE PINTS OF GUINNESS AND A SICK BUCKET FOR MY ENGLISH FRIEND.

Paralytic (adj)

(*see also* Bollixed Fluthered, Gee-eyed, Langered, Ossified, Plastered, Rat-arsed.)

So inebriated one actually passes out. *(usage) 'Do you know that it takes just four pints to get an Englishman paralytic?'*

Piss up (n)

Night of revelry and imbibing alcohol. *(usage) 'I must interrupt counsel's lengthy summation to remind him that the barristers' annual piss-up starts at five.'*

Plastered (adj)

(see also Bollixed, Fluthered, Gee-eyed, Langered, Ossified, Paralytic, Rat-arsed.)

Very drunk.
(usage) 'I was so plastered that the taxi-driver actually made sense.'

Puss (n)

Sulky face.
(usage) 'Frank had a puss on him just because me and the girls were watching Emmerdale during the World Cup Final.'

Rapid (adj)

Great. Fantastic. Amazing.
(usage) 'Yer mot's knockers are rapid.'

53

Rat-arsed (adj)

(see also Bollixed, Fluthered, Gee-eyed, Langered, Ossified, Paralytic, Rat-arsed)

Very drunk.
(usage) 'I was so rat-arsed I ate a spiceburger.'

Reddner (n)

Blush.
(usage) 'I'll tell ye, Mary, it was so small he had a reddner.'

Ride (n)(v)

(See also shag)

An attractive female or male. (v) To partake in sexual intercourse.
(usage) 'I had a ride of that ride in Accounts.'

Scanger (n)

(see also Scrubber, Slapper)

Female lacking in sophistication.
(usage) 'The scanger drank her finger bowl.'

Scarlet (adj)

(see also Mortified)

Embarrassed. Blushing.
(usage) 'I was scarlet
when I found out
afterwards that he
was a bishop.'

JAYSUS,
THAT WAS
GREAT!

Scratcher (n)

Bed.
(usage) 'If you're not
out of the scratcher
and here in ten minutes
operating on this man's
brain, you're fired.'

Scrubber (n)

(see also Scanger,
Slapper)

Woman of low moral
fibre and little
sophistication.
(usage) 'She's such a
scrubber that she
smokes during oral
sex.'

Scutters (n)

Diarrhoea.
(usage) 'Eight pints of Harp and a curry always gives my missus the scutters.'

Shag (v)

(see also Ride)

To have sexual intercourse.
(usage) 'That Viagra is great shaggin' stuff.'

Shattered (adj)

Very tired. Requiring sleep.
(usage) 'Listen, Taoiseach. The whole Cabinet's been working for nearly an hour and we're all shattered.'

Shenanigans (n)

Mischievous, suspicious, underhand, devious goings-on.
(usage) 'Next item on today's County Council agenda: planning shenanigans. Sorry, uh, planning submissions.'

Shite (adj)

Of extraordinarily poor quality.
(usage) 'The health service is shite.'

Shite hawk (n)

Swine. Pig. Scumbag.
(usage) 'When I asked that shite hawk Sean what we'd use for protection he said we could use de bus shelter.'

Shower of savages

(expression)

Loud, ignorant, unsophisticated crowd of people.
(usage) Q: 'Who's that shower of savages in the corner?'
A: 'That's the Cabinet.'

Single (n)

Bag of chips.
(usage) 'Micko was so good in bed I nearly dropped me single.'

Skiver (n)

Person who avoids honest work.
(usage) Kid: 'When I grow up I want to be a skiver like you, Dad.'
Dad: 'So you want to work in the insurance industry, then?'

Slag (v)

Make fun of a person in a lighthearted, friendly manner.
(eg) 'Yer a big ignorant sleeven of a muck savage, ye thick bogtrotter ye.'

Slapper (n)

Female of low morals and poor taste in clothing.
(usage) 'You're not really going to make that slapper a Minister, are you, Taoiseach?'

Slash (n) (v)

Urination.

(usage) ' ... if I may interrupt my learned friend, m'Lud, as I'm dying for a slash.'

Sleeveen (n)

Devious, sly, repulsive individual.
(eg) *Any member of Ireland's car insurance industry.*

Spondulicks (n)

Money.
(usage) 'Hee hee, gentlemen. Wait'll ye see the spondulicks our insurance company screwed out of Irish drivers last year.'

Suckin' diesel (now yer)
(expression)

Now you're talking! Now you're doing well!
(usage) 'Increase car insurance premiums by 20% for no reason? Now yer suckin' diesel, Mr Chief Executive!'

Thick (adj)

Extremely stupid.
*(eg) The person who
conceived RTE's
'Angelus' slot.*

Throw shapes (v)

To swagger excessively.
To show off.
*(usage) 'Will you stop
throwing shapes at those
slappers or we'll never
get a bleedin' shag.'*

Up the pole (expression)

With child. Pregnant.
*(usage) 'Great news,
Ma, I'm up de pole. I
mean, eh, engaged.'*

61

Wagon (n)

Unattractive female.
(usage) 'Better gimme
another pint. She still
looks like a wagon.'

Wojus (adj)

Extremely poor
quality.
(usage) 'The bus service,
the health service, the
train service, the telephone
service and every other
bleedin' government
service in Ireland is
wojus.'

Wrecked (adj)

Extremely tired.
Worn out.
(usage)   Ex-Civil
Servant : 'I'm wrecked
doing this ... what d'ye
call it?'
Private Employee: 'Work.'

Yard
(get up the) (expression)

Get lost!
*(usage) 'So, you drank
three quarters of it
before you realised it
was a bad pint?
Get up the yard!'*

Yer wan (n)

Female whose name
escapes one.
Nondescript individual.
*(usage) 'Yer wan over
there. Yeah, her. Me
wife.'*

You're wha? (expression)

Alleged method of
proposing to one's
sweetheart on
Dublin's northside.
*(usage) 'You're bleedin'
wha?'*

Yer man Colin Murphy in de picture is a wojus head-the-ball who's regularly paralytic from de gargle. He's a bit of a bowsie and he's always on de doss. His normal job is writin' ads but when he's not up to ninety with that, he likes to do a little nixer, like this. His English is ganky, which makes him de deadly choice to give dis a lash.

Considered by many to be an authority on Irish slang ever since he was a little gurrier, Donal O'Dea came to prominence when he became the first person to accurately differentiate between a scanger, a scrubber and slapper. He's been working in advertising for donkey's years and is believed by his colleagues to be a bit of a mentaller.

BOUT THE BOOK OF IRISH SONGS YER (
HOOLEY THE FECKIN' BOOK OF IRISH SE
THE BOOK OF LUVELY IRISH RECIPES '
RIER THE FECKIN' BOOK OF IRISH SAYIN
VER OF SAVAGES THE 2ND FECKIN' BOOI
FIRST ONE THE FECKIN' BOOK OF IRISH II
HALF AS USEFUL THE BOOK OF FECKI
RS AND BOWSIES THE BOOK OF DEADLY
IS ALWAYS BLATHERIN' ON ABOUT THE
WHEN HE WAS JARRED AT A HOOLEY TH
OR DACENT PEOPLE'S EYES THE BOOK
N YOU WERE A LITTLE GURRIER THE FEC
HE BATTER WITH A SHOWER OF SAVAGI
ES A HOLY SHOW OF THE FIRST ONE THI
HICK AS MANURE AND ONLY HALF AS US
AT CRAIC FOR CUTE HOORS AND BOWSIES
RT FECKER IN THE PUB IS ALWAYS BLATI
FELLA ALWAYS SANG WHEN HE WAS JA
& LOVE THAT'S NOT FIT FOR DACENT PEC
MA USETA MAKE WHEN YOU WERE A LITT
WHEN YOU GO ON THE BATTER WITH A
SLANG THAT MAKES A HOLY SHOW C
LTS FOR GOBDAWS AS THICK AS MAN
IN' IRISH SLANG THAT'S GREAT CRAIC F